f

Social History and Autonomy

an essay

This story is dedicated to book readers
who hunger for the truth

Lies evolve to become truths

Author: John Julius Candelaria

Born in Albuquerque, New Mexico. Earned a Bachelors Degree with majors in Psychology and Art from University of Albuquerque.

Other books by John Julius Candelaria:

Sara

Triad

Coma

Virion

Aminah

Sparrow

Panacea

Machine

Dementia

Mr. Kraus

Blue Seagull

Maggie's World

Proxima Centauri

CONTENTS:

____

FOREWORD

Absolutes cannot and do not exist. Wisdom whispers to each of us, "Truth for someone is a lie for another. Everything we witness using our eyes and our other four senses passes through filters which are unique to our individual self and our life experience." Higher wisdom adds, "Those filters which predicate anyone's life-experience can be sculpted individually or as a group by external forces." That process begins by manipulating the environment and the exposure of one person or an entire society. Within the dominion of mindless (non-reasoning) life-forms and systems, those realms are cared for and regulated by the force of Nature.

Autonomy is the hallmark of humanity; whence humankind is not governed by an omnipotent force as is lower-life. Rather, "we," being reasoning higher animals, rely on ourselves to regulate and maintain social order. Unbridled reason, if it was achievable, would proclaim that any life-form; singularly or as a group; or any system for that matter, cannot self-regulate as can be attested throughout recorded history. The most that any self-governing autonomous society can do to achieve a stable cooperative social state is to project an illusion of it being the ideal, and then record it. Depending on where anyone resides on this planet, their sociological history is distilled. Prior to the World-Wide-Web (WWW) coming into existence in 1990 history researcher's gathered and examined historical information by traveling to countries of interest. Upon compiling the history accounts of each country visited, researchers concluded: history is essentially myth; though researchers did not openly state that conclusion.

History in any form is a tool used to put forth credos of lies to maintain civil order and obedience. Social history content contained in any library is determined by the country where the library is located. Historical accounts which are researched at American libraries would be skewed toward the interest of America. That same bias applies to social history in a Chinese library or a Russian library, etc. It follows: due to the truth regarding social history being subjective, it means all history is collectively either altered or conjured.

Nature, on the other hand, truly operates flawlessly to maintain harmony and balance within the mindless (non-reasoning) dominion of all life below human life. Indeed, Nature does a fine job of running the universe but Nature remains removed from humanity. Autonomy is the hallmark of humankind; a dominion where Nature or any omnipotent force could not corral autonomous creatures. Hence, the absence of an all-serving governing force spells doom for "us."

Humanity cannot regulate its self for the reason we possess autonomous reasoning minds; whence each mind is a unique world. However, the human psyche is susceptible to manipulation; that much is clear when studying social history. And the proof is to simply perform a side-by-side comparison of each country's historical records found in libraries throughout the world.

It appears the only method for controlling a population's social behavior is by manufacturing webs of lies, propaganda, censorship, and abundances of elaborate falsehoods which are put forth as truths.

There is not any argument against Nature being the same absolute truth and reality for every creature and organism across the entire spectrum of life. However, as will be repeated throughout this essay, the essence of humankind is autonomy; a condition where truth is never certain for anyone individually or as a group. That *truth* is clear throughout the pages of historical records of any country.

Any rational person sees that the autonomous functionality of human society is inherently flawed due to its realm being inundated with lies. But can there be another way for a society to function in harmony and balance?

Perhaps not. The reason is because the human mind is a universe within itself and most people are incapable of dealing with such immensity. An analogy may be to place a pedestrian on the pilot's seat of a military aircraft, and launch the machine. The consequence of humans equipped with a complex universe to reason with is the fragile development of the human "psyche."

The personality of the human psyche is possibly more complicated than the universe. Every experience, beginning from birth, determines one's personality. When you lock eyes with any of 9 billion people on this planet you are peering at the most dangerous creature on Earth. A charging elephant is no match for a human with a gun, or a primitive tribe yielding spears.

That person whom you locked eyes with is also a jumble of confusion where everything they perceive passes through filters. Those subjective pathways alter any information before any level of assimilation takes place. Most of what gets through their filters is a plethora of untruths that gently stroke their fragile psyche...a mind that could erupt in any direction. Adding to all that is a possibility of one's mind having biological defects. The combination and consequences of all those factors spell danger.

It's mystifying why the human mind possesses such multifarious characteristics;

perhaps due to the penalty for having reasoning minds which re-shape the myriad of experiences humans perceive. The gain of reasoning autonomous minds is "we" are elevated to various intellectual planes. But what value is building grand cities and preparing to travel to the stars, whence social harmony and balance is unattainable?

Lower life is therefore vastly socially superior in every context and sphere of existence. Meanwhile, humankind plods along a path of falsehoods.

SECTION TWO

Books and documents lining the shelves or drawers of any library; whether the library is privately or municipally owned must first travel across the eyes of a curator's inherent bias desk before that information reaches the shelves. The largest library on this planet is the Library of Congress in Washington D.C. USA. It was established in 1880 and contains 170 million items. That grand library has curators who must approve any and all material held in that facility. Approval implies subjectivity, censorship and propaganda. Moreover, the journey of a historical parcel destined to line shelves of any library of any country was edited by numerous people before being passed on to library curators. One can only imagine the effects all those subjective minds had on a document before the parcel settled on a library shelf, if it made it there at all.

In this 21st Century, the World Wide Web serves as a global library where everyone can supposedly obtain accurate information about anything. But in fact; the WWW is just a collective macrocosm of any library where material is biased. That subjectivity determines everything which is accessible on the WWW. So who are those World Wide Web curators?

The first door where information must pass through on its subjective-based journey to the WWW and to our eyes and ears are internet service providers (ISPs). Their owners and curators approve or disallow any information a passageway to computers, and like devices, anywhere on this planet. From ISPs; the information pathway must next travel through WWW "search-engines." And again; material displayed on global computer devices must be approved by owners or CEOs of any search engine.

Social media is another informational-course strategy the WWW jointly employs to globally put forth biased news, promotions, education, connections, conversations, inspiration, entertainment and forums to discuss matters of social interest.

Google, Facebook, Twitter and Instagram are examples of social media platforms existing on the World Wide Web. Everything passing across them is carefully monitored by a small consortium of people before material if posted on the World Wide Web. Just as with libraries; anything not befitting the views of the social-media-mogul-curators who run WWW social networks never reaches "your" computer or device.

Hence, a hand full of "human personalities," sculpted by their distorted life experiences coordinate all material displayed on the World Wide Web. And those few biased people are in complete control of WWW internet providers, search engines, and social media platforms.

SECTION THREE

Interestingly; all censorship and propaganda on the WWW being spoon-fed to the global public, appears eerily similar to tactics of Nazi Germany during the late 1930s through mid 1940s.

Propaganda minister (more specifically: propaganda-censorship minister) Joseph Goebbels could be thought of as a microcosm of current social media moguls all wrapped into the psyche of Goebbels and the Nazi party.

If a journalist in 1940 Nazi Germany attempted to report views to the public that were not acceptable to the Nazi state, that journalist would be shot in a public square. His or her corpse would be skewered and propped up behind the speaking podium during a Nazi mass-rally. Upon studying all human history, it becomes clear that all political regimes exhibit some degree of conduct prevalent in Nazi Germany. Political and socialized behaviors are always connected to a central state-ideology that purports: social obedience and control. How those tactics are employed is expressed through various psychological methods. Ultimately, physical force is used to maintain the illusion of social harmony.

Curiously; Nature may utilize force in the form of natural phenomena such as weather geological stirring and even biological intervention to maintain balance and order of all lower life-forms. In spite of all that;

benefits reaped by mindless creatures, and the systems supporting their realm, are endless resources to sustain and perpetuate the mindless realm of lower animals.

Indeed, lower life and it supporting systems have been around since the beginning. Its realm has never exhibited any of the destructive and chaotic ways of humanity. Nature's dominion over lower-life and all its sustaining systems demonstrates unyielding order and balance.

Recognizing the dominion of Nature functions so perfectly, one could deduce: if humanity shed autonomy and became mind-less creatures that could not reason beyond basic needs, we too could achieve harmony and balance.

SECTION FOUR

A scheme Nature uses for perpetuating all lower life and systems is through "numbers." Examples of reproduction in numbers are Sea Turtles. They cyclically deposit millions of their eggs on certain beaches. Only a few offspring make it to adulthood; whence those few repeat that process. When all those nesting beaches become sites for golf courses and gambling casinos, Sea Turtles will become extinct. Or so it seems.

"Numbers" are also the hallmark of the universe. Anyone need only gaze up at a night sky where points of light appear to stretch to infinity and to where stars are born. Commonality is also part of the foundation of our universe...everything is connected. Those incalculable stars and galaxies in the heavens support countless Earth's due to the universal pattern of numbers...and those habitable planets are all likely just like our planet.

Further profundity of Nature is: Life in any form eventually dies. And someday when Earth becomes a Martian landscape, there are, after all, an abundance of planets just like this one "out there" where lower life and humanity may continue; presuming we can reach those oasis' before they too come to the end of their life, possible as a result of human interference.

Lower-life does not consume resources beyond what is needed to sustain its species.

Nature makes certain of that. The Human species does not follow that premise...not at all.

Humanity consumes more than it needs for its comfort and enjoyment, and various pleasures. Those actions disturb and threaten ours and Nature's dominion. So why then does nature provide elements that only humanity consumes and exploits?

There is not any other life-form, except humanity, that has need for oil and electricity and components to build nuclear devices which could diminish Earth to a Martian landscape. Why do components that could reduce Earth to a cinder exist?

Perhaps the structure of every habitable planet in the universe is composed of those elements. Since commonalities are shared by everything in this cosmos, one could ponder if consumption and depletion are necessary features of the universe's lifecycle. All life does indeed become depleted of its life-energy over time. At this instant, Earth's sun is depleting its energy, as are all stars in the universe doing the same.

If indeed, the cosmos mirrors life and death in the same manner as every living organism does, maybe the universe will someday perish and be reborn. If so, that explains many things, including our presence, and behavior. That behavior insures the demise of human habitats. Hence, the cycle of life and rebirth prevails; initially at the planetary level, and then happens everywhere in the universe.

The Greek philosopher Anaxagoras (500-428 B.C.) proposed that the seeds of life are commonly present everywhere in the universe. At the beginning of the 20th century, Svants Arrhenius' work won him the Nobel Prize for Chemistry in 1903. He asserted the "Panspermia theory." It states life on Earth was brought here in meteorites.

SECTION FIVE

The Panspermia theory generally states: life exists throughout the universe and spreads everywhere when space objects of any kind collide and its elements are dispersed to other space objects. And then, those objects collide or explode, further dispersing seeds of life-forms, including human seeds, across the universe.

Eventually, any habitable planet; either during its early formation or later, collects space-debris which is laden with "all" life-forms. Those life-forms then become established and flourish on a suitable planet.

The comets cited in the Panspermia theory imply the universe came about after a violent explosion that propelled comets and other debris away from the blast and throughout the cosmos. The commonality of all things conjures a dire possibility. Science believes Earth is a "newborn" in relation to the age of the universe. If that is so; that means all life-supporting planets have been annihilated due to the scourge humanity leashed upon them by exhausting their resources. More importantly than us depleting Nature's resources is the matter of social unrest due to autonomy. The results which could be wars that annihilate everything on this planet.

Therefore; it could be reasoned that Earth is the only habitable planet left in a spent cosmos. Thus, this planet and its populations are the final chapter of life in any form in the entire universe.

The truth about human social history and its inevitable fate is this story — higher life ultimately, not only destroys its biological host, humankind also lays waste to the imperial host of everything...the universe.

But I, as a human, cannot conclude this story by damning and condemning humankind because I, after all, am one of you. Suppose then, in the mysterious realm of infinity where time never ends, Nature may have evolved over the many cycles of birth and rebirth of this universe...likely not.

Perhaps the evolving Nature has adapted to the ever-presence of humankind on livable planets. So, change may happen to prolong the life span of Earth. Surely, Nature could desire to extend "its" life.

And the way all that comes about is if humanity achieves peace and harmony. The first step toward that direction begins with social behavior; whence the World Wide Web, social media and world and local news open the gates of total knowledge for all to know the consequences of conflicting social ideologies as the harbingers of Earth's demise.

The next chapter of this essay covers "societal-rule" ideologies which anyone with an open and unbiased mind may untangle to arrive at unbridled historical social truth. Thenupon, Earth's population can express not individual autonomy, but social autonomy, whence 9 billion higher life-forms are on a single common course.

SECTION SIX

Fundamental to animals is the alpha-male that rules a group. That practice is also common to higher animals (mindful-autonomous-reasoning creatures). However, the intrinsic alpha-male characteristic evolved in higher life-forms. This section examines nine types of rule which evolved from when the first human alpha-male kept order among a group, to the present.

♦ Overlords emerged from within small human groups. The overlords were basically dominant alpha-males. They took charge and maintained order within groups of people. Overlords exist today in many parts of the world. Some strive to maintain stability within a community. Or, an overlord may lead rebel bands whose aim is to topple the "establishment" in some kind of religious context; as in Middle East disruptor groups.

♦ The first Monarch ruling structure appeared in Egypt around 4000 B.C. Pharaohs were deemed as theocratic monarchs; whereby, the king ruled by a mandate of the divine. That form of rule maintained societal harmony for thousands of years. More recent Monarchs, such as what existed in Britain prior to 1215 are now parliaments. They are essentially republics and democracies; whence a country is ruled by the people via elected officials. The King or Queen is merely figureheads whom do not make political decisions.

♦ Capitalism means: privately owned competitive markets with its own price system which yields profits. In many ways, the United States of America functions like a monarch society but without the family royalty associated in British Monarchy. And as with British monarchy, the American president is a figurehead. However, a USA president can make political decisions but at a very limited level.

♦ Dictatorship is absolute rule by one person and a party using forcible suppression, repression, cruelty or whatever means to control a society toward the whims of the dictator. Fascism is dictatorial with a central xenophobic ideology of race dominance (racial hatred).

♦ Socialism rules the populous as an ideological system that shares the economy equally throughout the population. It promotes collective well-being of the community rather than individuals. The government distributes resources, giving it greater control over its citizens. Socialism advocates the elimination of class distinction and conformity.

♦ Communism is both a dictatorial government and a socialistic ideology; whereby the people collectively own all production as determined by a dictator at the expense of people's liberty. "Communist Manifesto" is a Karl Mark doctrine published in 1848. Marx proposed a utopian society based on a classless society. His manifesto set forth 2 stages needed to achieve utopia. First: a revolution was needed to overthrow the existing regime and completely eradicate the old system. Second: a dictator must come to power and act as the sole authority on all matters including the personal matters of the public. Mark's utopia never came to fruition.

♦ Capitalism is essentially a free-market system where government benefits from gains of the masses. Class distinctions are the result of the rich having a great deal of wealth, and the middle class having some, and the lowest caste has very little. Meanwhile, Socialism raps on the door of Capitalism but those knocks are ignored.

♦ Imperialism and Colonialism follow the same tenet: conquer, exploit, subjugate the indigenous population, and essentially "move in" to any geographical locale. During the lifetime of any geographical parcel of living space on this planet, the people residing there have experienced Colonialism-Imperialism.

♦ Autocracy is rule by one person. Nazi Germany was an example of that system.

♦ Anarchism is an ideology whereby a complete absence of rule exists. No time in history has that ideology been a functioning society in higher or lower animals.

Plants and even microbes operate by rules. Nature's rule maintains biological and natural conformity throughout all the mindless species of living organisms.

Upon examining the above nine principles of social rule, one can deduce that historical evidence and what we know from using our five senses and power of reasoning; only Nature's dominion results in balance, harmony, and order. History's second truth is that social disorder and war has prevailed from since higher-life first appeared on this planet. Could the conclusion for predicting "our" fate be: Humanity is doomed, and we will also doom this planet?

SECTION SEVEN

●

This universe is a living organism and humanity is a component of it, otherwise we would not exist. We have not yet discovered our role, but there absolutely is one. The focus of this essay is not to determine our role in the grand scheme of it all; but that topic will be addressed in another essay. For now, I will continue the essay-topic.

●

Being a living organism, this universe has to die sometime. And just as all things return to live again, when this universe comes to its end and then restarts with an explosive force, we also shall return...as how Panspermia suggests.

Also onboard the shrapnel coming from the re-birth of this universe, will be mindless "seeds" of life along side us. The shrapnel will be in the form of comets and asteroids and space debris and will sail all across the universe with its cargo of seeds-of-life. When the cosmos stabilizes, a newly formed universe appears from all that chaos. Eventually, microscopic seeds that have been passengers of space debris for incalculable eons find their way to habitable planets.

The advantage goes to lower life because mindless organisms have the omnipotent force of Nature on their side which establishes balance and order among all mindless life. But human mindful-life must fend for itself. So, without its own omnipotent force to govern autonomous creatures, floundering humankind acts out with inherent individual independence. All attempts to self-regulate fail. And just as in the previous universe, humanity collects in groups.

Alpha males emerge and the cycle of governing ideologies develop. Social factions divide, and then form societies. Geographical spacing between societal groups creates cultural-behaviors. Next, comes formations of caste-divisions within societies. And then, opportunistic overlords with persuasive powers, and in possession of resources such as wealth draw followers. Those followers create politics of an ideology.

Eventually, entire countries come under ideologically-based rule. Being intrinsically autonomous, humanity resists conformity. The leader and their party firstly apply propaganda and censorship to maintain civil order and obedience. When societies coalesce and come under complete control, the leader and his party expand their ideology beyond their borders. That imperialistic process brings about conflict and discord — and once again, the intrinsic component of autonomy is expressed.

Societies beyond country borders follow their own ideology; hence, force is used to make those societies submit...escalating war is the result. When global war ensues, it is most interesting that societies and countries of differing social values unite to squash the principal disrupting warring source. The spoils of war are divided among the victors. After-affects of differing ideologies of the victors create further contentions that become highly complex and irresolvable.

Psychological battles rage between societies and countries as propaganda and censorship attempt to overturn conflicting ideologies that have become so muddled, they are hardly indistinguishable from each other.

The non-conforming characteristic of humanity increasingly creates greater and greater discontent. During all that while, time has crept slowly forward and humanity achieves technology which brings about a new method to suppress and advance ideologies on a global scale.

SECTION EIGHT

There is a solution to every dilemma. The solution is always to eliminate the dilemma.

ARE WE TO BE CONTINUED?

Social History and Autonomy

an essay

NOTES: